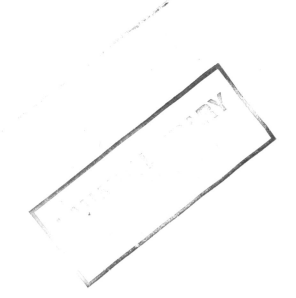

THE
FARMER
THROUGH HISTORY

Peter Chrisp

with illustrations by Tony Smith

Wayland

JOURNEY THROUGH HISTORY

The Farmer Through History
The Inventor Through History
The Sailor Through History
The Soldier Through History

Series editor: William Wharfe
Editor: Margot Richardson
Designer: Robert Wheeler

Typeset in the UK by Dorchester
Typesetting Group Ltd
Printed in Italy by G. Canale &
C.S.p.A., Turin

First published in 1992 by
Wayland (Publishers) Limited
61 Western Road, Hove
East Sussex BN3 1JD, England

© Copyright 1992 Wayland
(Publishers) Limited

**British Library Cataloguing in
Publication Data**
Chrisp, Peter
  Farmer Through History – (Journey
  Through History Series)
  I. Title II. Smith, Tony III. Series
  630.7

ISBN 0-7502-0384-6

Text acknowledgements
The publishers have attempted to
contact all copyright holders of the
quotations in this book, and
apologize if there have been any
oversights.
The publishers gratefully
acknowledge permission from the
following to reproduce copyright
material: Hamlyn Publishing, for an
extract from *Myths and Legends of
Ancient Egypt*, by TGH James, 1969;
Heinemann (Loeb Classical Library),
for extracts from: 1) WD Hooper's
translation of Cato's *De Agricultura*,
1934, 2) WD Hooper's translation of
Varro's *De Agricultura*, 1934, 3) H
Rackham's translation of Pliny's
Natural History, 1950; Open
University Press, for an extract from
HS Bennett's version of *Pierce the
Ploughman's Creed*, quoted in
*Economy and Society in Western
Europe 1300-1600*, 1971; Penguin
Books Ltd, for an extract from *Out of
the Ancient World*, by Victor Skipp,
1967; Routledge and Kegan Paul, for
extracts from: 1) *Great Benin: Its
Customs, Art and Horrors*, by HL
Roth, 1968, 2) *The History of a
Soviet Collective Farm*, by Fedor
Belov, 1956.

Picture acknowledgements
The publisher wishes to thank the
following for supplying photographs
for use as illustrations in this book:
Ancient Art & Architecture
Collection 17; CM Dixon 9, 13, 14,
16, 25; ET Archives *cover*, 12, 20, 24,
33, 37; Michael Holford 6, 9, 10, 20,
29, 33; The Hutchison Library 4, 5,
21, 30; Novosti Press Agency 38, 40,
41; Ann Ronan Picture Library 34,
36; Zefa Picture Library 22, 42. All
other pictures are in the Wayland
Picture Library.

Contents

From hunter gatherers to farmers

From the earliest times people have fed themselves by hunting animals and gathering fruits, nuts and vegetables growing in the wild. People have been living on earth for at least 200,000 years, but it is only in the last 10,000 years that they have discovered how to produce food for themselves by farming.

Today, in some parts of the world, like rainforests, hunting and gathering continues to be a very effective way of finding food. However, about 9,000 years ago, people in a very different landscape began to use a new way of making sure that they had enough to eat. They started growing their favourite plants and tending them until they produced fruit. They started to keep and breed certain animals, eating them when they wanted to, instead of having to hunt them. They had started to farm.

No one knows exactly why people first started to farm. The switch from gathering to farming was probably very slow. For a long time, the two ways of life were combined. Learning to farm was a complicated process. People had to work out the best way to dig the earth and to sow, harvest and store their crops. This called for knowledge of the different seasons of the year, when to sow and when to harvest, and how much grain to keep in reserve for the next year's sowing. They also had to domesticate, or tame, wild animals: goats and sheep, and later cattle.

The Uru Eu Wau Wau people of Brazil still live successfully as hunters and gatherers. But farming has slowly replaced this way of life throughout the world.

4

At first, these were just kept for meat. But, in time, people discovered how to milk them and use wool. People then started to use animals to pull the plough and work machinery.

Farming ensured a regular supply of food. This meant that people could settle down in one place. Farming could produce more food than was needed, so this could be traded for other goods or used to support craftspeople. Villages grew into towns which grew into cities.

Through farming, people were able to control the world around them better than before. Gradually, over a long time, they changed animals and plants by selecting the healthiest and biggest ones for breeding. They also changed the landscape, draining swamps and clearing forests. But, in many ways, people were still at the mercy of nature. Bad weather, disease and pests could destroy crops and animals. The early farmers saw these disasters, as well as the movement of the seasons, as the work of unseen forces. Increasingly, people turned to new religions to try to win over these unseen forces to their side.

Goat and cattle farmers in modern Kenya. Through taming and then herding wild animals, people could control their supply of meat, and also use animals for milk.

A new coat
Wild sheep have a hairy outer coat, and a fine woolly down between the hairs. Once sheep had been domesticated, people began to breed animals with more of this down, until they grew a thick woolly fleece. Animals, like plants, were changed by farming.

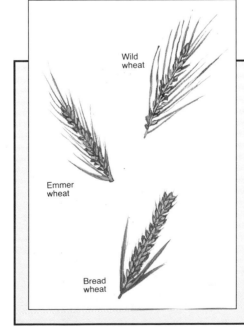

Wild wheat

Emmer wheat

Bread wheat

A new kind of wheat
In its wild form, wheat has an ear which shatters easily, so that its grains can be carried by the wind. The first farmers selected plants with the biggest, toughest ears, for they were easier to gather. As a result of this selection, wheat slowly changed. New forms appeared with bigger grains, such as einkorn and emmer. The final development was bread wheat, which has grains fixed to the stem. It cannot spread its seeds without help from humans.

A farmer in Jericho

One of the first farming communities in the world was that of Jericho in the Jordan valley in the Middle East. Jericho was the perfect place for farming. There is a permanent spring there that still produces over 4,000 litres of water every minute. This was an oasis in a hot dry land, a place where wild grasses grew and gazelles and goats grazed.

In 7000 BC, Jericho was a small town. It covered an area of 3 to 4 hectares and was surrounded by a stone wall. It had a population of between two and three thousand people, fed by the food provided by farming.

The people of Jericho grew barley and two types of wheat – emmer and einkorn – as well as peas and lentils. They cleared and dug the fields with simple hoes and harvested the grain with sickles made of flints, mounted in deer horn or wood. The grain was kept in storage pits and ground into flour on a large flat stone called a saddle quern. It was then made into a kind of simple bread. There were also goats for milk and for meat, and people hunted gazelles and foxes, using bows and arrows.

Bricks of mud

The Jericho farmers used bricks made of dried mud to build their houses, which were small and circular. The floors in the houses were covered with woven rush mats, and people slept on raised clay benches.

One of the oldest buildings in the world, the 9-metre-high stone tower of Jericho, uncovered by an archaeological dig.

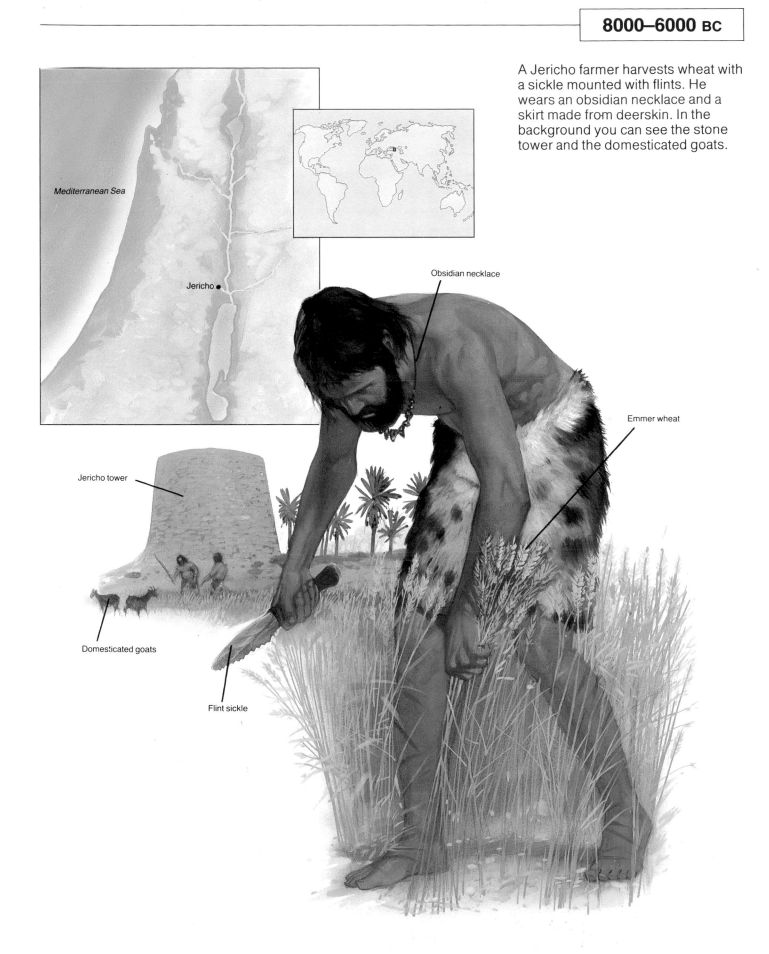

A Jericho farmer harvests wheat with a sickle mounted with flints. He wears an obsidian necklace and a skirt made from deerskin. In the background you can see the stone tower and the domesticated goats.

Mediterranean Sea

Jericho

Obsidian necklace

Emmer wheat

Jericho tower

Domesticated goats

Flint sickle

A farmer in Jericho

The farmers of Jericho lived between 8000 and 6000 BC. They could not write and so they left no descriptions of how they lived. Yet, thanks to archaeologists, we know many things about them.

The houses in Jericho were built of mud brick. When the mud brick was old and began to crumble the houses were knocked down. The old brick was not thrown away; instead it was used to repair streets and floors. The layers of brick gradually built up over the years, creating a mound or *tell*. By digging into this mound, the archaeologists could uncover layer on layer of streets, floors and houses. The deeper they dug, the further back into the past they travelled. Towards the bottom of the mound they found the houses and tools of some of the first farmers in the world. They found large numbers of flints, with a glossy shine on them which only comes from harvesting grasses. They also found the twisted horns of domesticated goats (wild goats in this area had curved horns).

The finds at Jericho showed the effect of farming on life. The first people who lived in Jericho were not farmers, but hunters and gatherers. There were not very many of them, because hunting and gathering could not support a large number. It was not until people started farming that the town grew.

Producing more food than they needed, the Jericho people were able to sell it to other people in exchange for items they could not make themselves. Archaeologists found cowrie shells (used like beads in jewellery) from the Red Sea, and obsidian (a hard volcanic glass used for making knives and jewellery) from Cliftik, southern Turkey. These were brought to Jericho through trade.

Flour and bread

Once cereals (wheat, barley, oats) have been harvested, they have to be threshed, which means beating the grass until the grains separate from the stalks and husks.

Then the grain is winnowed – tossed in the air until the heavier grains fall to the ground, and the light straw and husks, or chaff, are blown away. The grains can then be ground into flour. Water is mixed with the flour to produce a dough, which, when baked, produces bread.

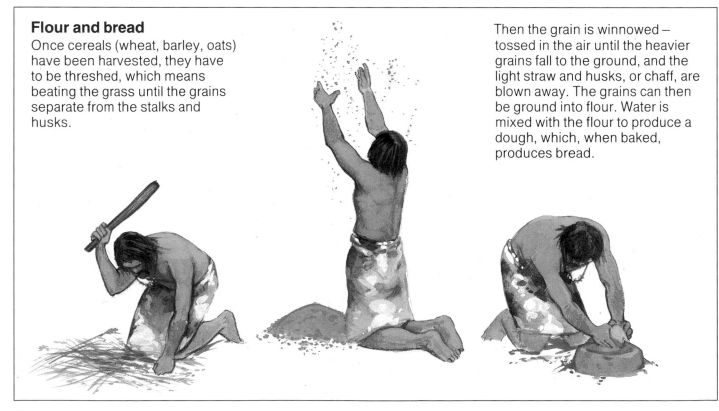

Jericho was protected by large walls and a tall tower, which were regularly repaired and enlarged. This shows that the Jericho farmers must have had some form of government in order to organize the work. It also shows that the Jericho people feared other people, who probably lived in similar towns. Farming meant that the people of Jericho had something to protect. Their fertile oasis must have been envied by less successful farmers, or by wandering bands of hunters. Farming, then, led to the beginnings of government and also perhaps of warfare.

The archaeologists also found tiny clay models of women and animals. Similar models of women have been found in many of the early farming settlements. They are often thought to be statues of an earth goddess, a figure who made the crops grow and protected the animals. But it is possible that they were just children's toys.

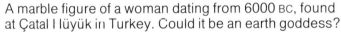
A marble figure of a woman dating from 6000 BC, found at Çatal Hüyük in Turkey. Could it be an earth goddess?

Ancestor worship?
The strangest thing about the people of Jericho was the way they buried the dead. The head was removed from the dead body, and stripped down to the skull. It was then covered with clay, moulded and painted so that it looked like the person it had belonged to. Perhaps this was a form of ancestor worship: some peoples believe that, after death, grandparents and parents continue to watch over a family. This is literally what the dead of Jericho did. The decorated skulls were kept on display in the houses.

One of the skulls found at Jericho. Most of the clay showing the features has fallen away. The eyes are two shells.

An Egyptian peasant farmer

Most ancient Egyptians were peasant farmers, working their own small plots of land or labouring on the huge fields of the estates owned by the king, the nobles and the temples of Egypt's gods.

It hardly ever rained in Egypt and most of the land was desert. Farming was only possible because once a year the River Nile flooded. Every July, the great river would rise, and for over three months the fields would be covered with water. All farming had to stop. When the water level sank, in November, it would leave behind a layer of rich black mud. The river also left behind a lot of water trapped in basins, or reservoirs. These were dug by the farmers so that they could water the crop later. When the water went down the hard work would begin.

The first task was to mark out the edges of the fields with small mud walls. Then the peasants would clear the channels along which the water would flow to the fields. Then the seeds – wheat and barley – would be scattered and turned into the soil with a plough, or trodden in by cattle.

In March, the crops were ready to be harvested. This was the busiest time in the peasants' year, as they worked from sunrise to night. After the harvest, the land would dry up under the hot summer sun, waiting for the Nile to rise again.

Cattle power

With the invention of the plough and the use of cattle to pull it, farming took a giant step forward. Now farmers could grow a crop on a field rather than a small plot. The Egyptians used a light wooden plough, or ard, which only turned the topmost level of soil, the black mud left by the river. Below this level lay the desert sand.

A model of a ploughing scene, placed in a nobleman's tomb around 2000 BC.

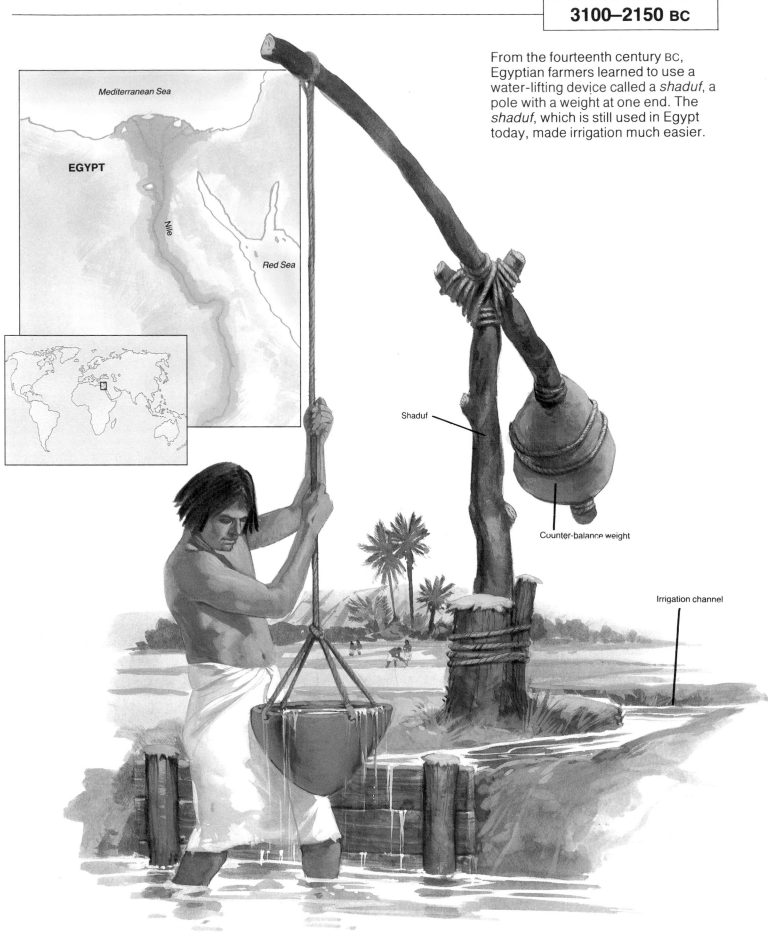

From the fourteenth century BC, Egyptian farmers learned to use a water-lifting device called a *shaduf*, a pole with a weight at one end. The *shaduf*, which is still used in Egypt today, made irrigation much easier.

Mediterranean Sea

EGYPT

Nile

Red Sea

Shaduf

Counter-balance weight

Irrigation channel

The yearly flooding of the Nile affected every part of Egyptian life. The people knew that their lives depended on the mysterious rise of the river, and on the black mud it left behind. They called their country *Keme*, which means 'the black land' (the modern name comes from the Greek word for the country: *Aigyptos*). Beyond the narrow strip of fertile soil lay the desert.

The flooding always happened at the same time, but the river did not always rise the same amount. If the river did not rise high, there might not be enough water for the crops and there would be a famine. And if the Nile rose too high the water would break the dykes; villages and grain stores could be flooded and the livestock drowned. The Egyptians did not know that the flooding was caused by rain in mountains far to the south. They thought it was caused by the gods. They also believed that it was not the river that sank at the end of the flood season, but that a new land every year magically rose from the water.

The king of Egypt, the pharaoh, was himself thought to be a god. Everyone and everything in Egypt belonged to the pharaoh. It was believed

This tomb painting shows all the different stages of harvesting. After the wheat has been harvested with curved sickles, it is trodden by oxen to separate the grain from the chaff. Then it is winnowed by being tossed in the air.

A peasant's life

The hard life of a peasant farmer is described in an ancient Egyptian school text:

The farmer wears the same clothes all the time. His fingers are always busy, his arms are dried up by the wind. He rests, when he is able, in the mud. If he is ill, his bed is the bare earth in the middle of his beasts. He scarcely gets home at night before he has to start off again.

Watering the crops

The Egyptians were experts at irrigation – controlling the supply of water to dry fields. They built earth walls, or dykes, to protect their villages and gardens from the rising river. From the reservoirs, they built canals to carry the water with its rich silt to outlying areas. Thanks to irrigation, the Egyptians were able to reclaim some of the desert for farming.

that he could make sure that the Nile continued to flood. The pharaoh's coronation traditionally took place on the day the river started to rise. During the flood season, he would sail in a state barge down the river and perform ceremonies believed to control its height. Even after the pharaoh's death, it was thought that he continued to protect the land in the next life. This was why the Egyptians took such care when they built pyramids, the huge royal tombs made of stone. Inside the pyramids the Egyptians placed everything the pharaoh would need after death, in the other world.

Because people needed to know when the Nile would flood, they invented a calendar. By knowing exactly what the date was, they would then know when the floods were due. The Egyptians noticed that every year, the star Sirius appeared in the sky just as the Nile began to rise. This was taken as the start of the Egyptian year. Years of observing and recording the daily level of the river eventually resulted in a 365-day calendar.

The Egyptians divided the year into three seasons

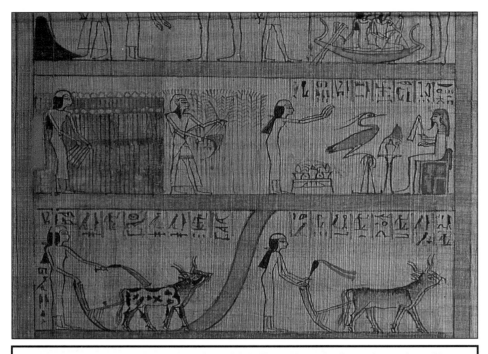

A farming scene in the afterlife, which Egyptians believed was just like their own land of Egypt. They reasoned that, like Egypt, the afterlife would have a river flowing through it to make farming possible.

Gods of the Nile

The Egyptians believed that the gods made the Nile flood. In an inscription on an island in the upper Nile, the god *Khnum* speaks: *I am Khnum, your maker. I am the great creator lord who orders everything. I am the Nile in flood who runs at will. My sanctuary [home] has two gates from which I can let out the water for the flood. It is the flood that brings life to everyone. Everything it irrigates continues to live.*

– *akhet*, the time of the flood; *perit*, the time of planting and growth; and *shomu*, the time of harvest and drought. Most of the farm work took place during *perit*, the second season. But this does not mean that the peasants could relax for the rest of the year. In the other seasons, particularly during the time of the flood (*akhet*) they were likely to be made to join labour gangs, hauling stone for the construction of the

pyramids or building irrigation canals.

At harvest time royal tax inspectors would arrive to measure the standing crops and work out how much tax the farmers should pay. Money had not been invented, so taxation took the form of a proportion of the grain. As much as half was taken to fill the royal stores. This was needed to feed the rest of the population of Egypt. Everybody depended on the work of the farmers.

A Roman slave farmer

Farming in ancient Italy often took place on great estates called *latifundia*. These were owned by rich Romans who might farm them themselves, or let them out to tenants. The real work was done by slaves – people who had been captured by the Romans in wars or were born of slave parents. A slave was treated, along with the farm animals, as part of the farm stock.

Conditions for the slaves varied according to their job. At the top was the *vilicus*, or steward, who ran the farm from day to day. By loyal service, a steward might eventually be rewarded with his freedom. Below him were the foremen of the field gangs. At the bottom were the field labourers. Their work was hard and continued all year round. Even when there was no farming to be done, they would be kept busy. They could be punished by being chained up or beaten. But it was in the farmer's interest to keep the slaves healthy. Like his farm animals, slaves cost money.

A slave's life

Roman farming manuals often offered advice on the treatment of slaves.

Sell worn-out oxen, blemished sheep, an old wagon, old tools, an old slave, a sickly slave, and whatever else is no longer needed. Cato (234–149 BC), (*On Agriculture* 11,7)

Slaves should be neither timid nor high spirited. They ought to have men over them who are dependable. Avoid having too many slaves of the same nation, for this is a fertile source of domestic quarrels. Varro (116–27 BC), (*On Agriculture* 1,17)

This mosaic from Tunisia shows the comfortable life of the rich on a big farming estate in North Africa. In the top row, the mistress of the house is offered some of the newly harvested olives. In the middle row, the master sets off on a hunting trip. At the bottom, the master and mistress are shown again: the mistress taking her jewellery from a household slave, the master watching over the fruit harvest.

ROMAN EMPIRE

Britain
Germany
Gaul
Italy
Greece
Rome
Syria
Spain
Mediterranean Sea
Africa
Egypt

Estate owner

Slave using stick to beat tree

Fallen olives

Watched over by the rich owner of the estate, the slaves harvest the olives by beating the trunks and branches of the trees.

In AD 117, the Roman Empire was at its greatest extent. It included almost all the lands around the Mediterranean Sea and stretched from Spain to Turkey and from Britain to Egypt – 4,000 km east to west and 3,700 km north to south. The Romans' success in warfare provided the wealthy farmers with a steady supply of slaves to work on the estates. Thanks to the conquest of Egypt (55 BC) and north Africa (146–44 BC), the city of Rome was able to import enough

Corn being loaded on a merchant ship. This wall painting comes from Ostia, the port through which most of Rome's grain was carried.

grain to allow free supplies to all the people who lived there (over a million people lived in Rome).

Despite their success in warfare and the wealth it brought, the Romans never forgot that they were a farming people. For a rich Roman, owning a farm was the only respectable way of making money. The most powerful Roman families owned great farming estates. Romans remembered that many of their best soldiers and generals had also been farmers. One of their greatest heroes was Cincinnatus who, in 458 BC, was called from ploughing his small farm to

lead Rome's armies against foreign invaders. Once he had defeated them, he went back to his farm.

The Romans believed that their gods could ensure a good harvest. They would pray to the goddess Ceres, from whose name the word 'cereal' is derived. But they also prayed to other gods. Mars, the god of war, was also a god of the spring and of agriculture. The most powerful god, Jupiter, was a weather god who presided over the sowing of seeds and watched over the boundary stones in the fields. Saturn was a god of the vines and watched over the manuring of the fields.

We know a lot about Roman agriculture thanks to farming manuals written by wealthy Romans such as Cato, Varro and Columella. These have detailed instructions on how to run a farm, and advice on which gods to pray to at each stage of the farming year.

The Romans knew that mixed farming, in which the fields for growing crops are fertilized by animal manure, was the best method. Cato described the ideal farm as having fields for grain, pasture for animals, a vineyard and an olive grove. He also recommended willows for baskets, meadows for hay, trees for timber, an orchard for fruit, an oak wood to provide acorns for pigs and a garden. However, mixed farming was not always possible. In Italy, the farmers had to adapt to a climate with autumn and winter rains, and a long drought in the summer. During the summer drought, sheep and cattle might have to be taken away from the estate to distant pastures. Without the animals' manure, some land would have to be left alone each year so that it would remain fertile.

A harvesting machine

On the latifundia in the province of Gaul, very large frames, fitted with teeth at the edge, and carried on two wheels, are driven through the corn by a pack animal pushing from behind. The ears thus torn off fall into the frame. Pliny the Elder (AD 23–79), (*Natural History* 18, 296)

A Roman mosaic showing a man ploughing with two oxen.

Sacrifice

The main religious festival of the farming year was the *Ambarvalia*, held every May. A pig, a sheep and a bull would be led in procession around the fields and then sacrificed to Mars, god of farming as well as war. This was thought to protect the fields from evil influences.

A Mayan maize farmer

A large part of Central America is tropical rainforest. There it rains heavily from May until October and is hot and dry for the rest of the year. In AD 500, this was the land of the Mayas. The Mayas practised a type of farming called 'slash and burn', which involves clearing an area of forest and burning it. The farmer would clear his *milpa*, or plot, in the autumn, using a stone axe. After the wood and brush had dried out under the hot sun of February and March, it would be burned. The ashes left after the burning helped to fertilize the soil. From April to July, the Mayas would plant maize in the ashes using a fire-hardened, pointed digging stick. The maize would grow during the rainy months and was ready for harvesting from November to April.

For two to three years, the *milpa* would be very productive. But the Mayas did not use ploughs, so weeds would start to take over; and each year's crop would take more goodness from the soil until it was exhausted. This was when they would clear a new area of forest. After ten years, the exhausted land would have recovered and could be cleared again.

Farming maize

Maize, like wheat, is a plant that has been changed by people. Once it had tiny cobs, covered with a thin husk that opened to let the seeds drop to the ground. But as people selected plants with bigger cobs, maize was slowly altered. The cobs became tightly wrapped in a thick husk and firmly fixed to the stalk of the plant. This made the maize easier to harvest.

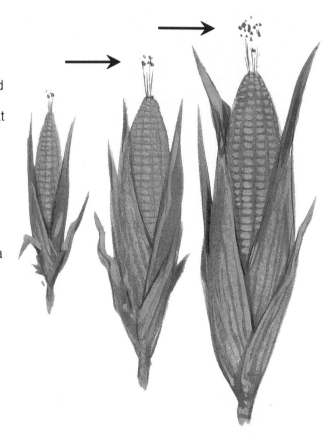

A Mayan meal

Maize is an excellent source of carbohydrate and fat, foods which we all need for energy. But maize is lacking in vitamins and protein (the basic building block of all human cells). Fortunately, the Mayas also grew beans, planted in the same holes as the maize and growing around its stalks. Beans, a rich source of protein and vitamins, combined with maize to form a balanced diet. The beans also helped to keep the soil fertile, because bean plants help to keep nutrients in the soil.

Gulf of Mexico

YUCATAN REGION

Pacific Ocean

Stone axe

Pointed digging sticks

Mayan farmers clear a new *milpa*, or
corn field, using stone axes.

A Mayan maize farmer

Chacs, the gods of rain. The Mayas would also make offerings of their own blood, by piercing their tongues with thorns. Maize itself was worshipped as a god. It was thought of as a young man with long hair, like the hairs, or silks, on an ear of maize.

Only the priests would be allowed into the temples and they would perform religious ceremonies high on the temple platform. The farmers believed that these ceremonies would bring a good maize harvest. The priests studied the movements of stars and

The ancient Mayas are best known for their beautiful stone cities, like Chichen Itzá, built deep in the jungles of the Yucatan region of Central America. These cities were religious centres and each was dominated by a temple, often more than 60 m tall. Yet it was only thanks to the work of the farmers that the cities could exist. The rulers, priests and craftsmen who lived there depended on food paid as a tax by the farmers.

The farmers would visit the cities, bringing food to offer the gods of the sun, the wind, and the four

The temple area of the Mayan city, Chichen Itzá, showing the pyramid shaped temple in the background. In the foreground is a stone jaguar, an animal sacred to warriors throughout Central America.

Chocolate
The Mayas grew cacao trees for the cocoa beans. Some of these were ground up to make a bitter chocolate drink (the word chocolate comes from the Aztec word *xocolatl*, meaning 'bitter water'). Other cocoa beans were used as a form of money.

A stone figure of the Mayan god of maize, who was thought of as a young man. Unlike many of the Mayan gods, the maize god was always seen as a friend to the people.

planets. They could predict the movements of the Moon, the Sun and the planet Venus. They also invented a calendar, the most accurate calendar in the world at that time. Thanks to the calendar, the priests could predict the rainy season. They would tell the farmers when to clear or burn the *milpa*.

Decline of the Mayas

In the ninth century, the Mayan cities went into a mysterious decline. The great building work stopped, the cities were abandoned and the calendar, knowledge of mathematics and writing were all lost. The Mayas survived (they still live in the region today), but archaeologists discovered that in about AD 850 the Mayan population suddenly fell. No one knows why this happened, though many theories have been suggested, from disease to foreign invasion.

It may have been the *milpa* method itself that was to blame. Successful slash-and-burn farming needs a large area of land. If there were too many people in one area, there would not be enough land left to make new *milpas*. With less forest to use, the farmers would be forced to shorten the period the *milpas* were left fallow before they were used again. At first, this might produce more maize, but it would leave the soil infertile. There may have been a long famine, when many people died of hunger.

Cattle and horses were not introduced to Central America until the sixteenth century, so the Mayas had no animals suitable for helping them out with farm work such as ploughing. The only animals they domesticated were turkeys, ducks and dogs. The dogs were not pets or used for hunting. Instead, they were fattened on maize and eaten or sacrificed to the

In Central America, people still make *tortillas* in the traditional way, grinding the specially prepared maize between two stones, patting the dough flat (seen here), and then cooking the *tortilla* over the fire.

gods. The Mayas also kept stingless bees for their honey. The bees were kept in hollow logs enclosed with mud at one end.

Preparing and cooking the maize was done by the women. It was dried, husked and boiled with a mixture of ashes until it was soft. Then it was mixed with water and ground into paste on a mill stone. The paste or dough was then rolled flat and heated over the fire. Mexicans still eat maize in a similar way; the pancakes are called *tortillas*.

A Chinese rice farmer

In the eleventh century, the Yangtze river of China was the centre of a vast farming area. The main crop was wet rice, the only cereal with roots that thrive under water. The land was farmed by peasant families, often on great estates owned by the government or by rich landowners.

The peasants had to work almost all the year round. In April, they would prepare the paddy field, repairing dykes and banks. The field would then be flooded with water pumped up or channelled from rivers, lakes or specially made reservoirs. A water buffalo would be used to pull the plough, guided by a farmer whose feet would sink into the wet mud with every step.

The rice seed was first sown in beds. In May, seedlings (young plants) were selected and planted in the paddy fields. The farmer could then be sure that almost all the rice plants in the paddy field would grow. The whole family would do the planting. The seedlings would be individually pushed into the mud in rows. This was very hard work which called for constant stooping.

About 100 days later, the rice would be ready for harvesting and the field would be drained. Harvesting was done by hand, using sickles and billhooks. After the harvest, the whole process would begin again. The peasants could grow two or even three crops of rice every year.

Farming silk

One of the greatest Chinese discoveries was the making of silk, from threads spun by the caterpillar of the silk moth. The caterpillars are bred on open trays and fed on mulberry leaves. After feeding for a month, they spin their fine silken cocoons, which are unravelled, spun and woven into cloth. To feed the caterpillars, there were orchards of mulberry trees, which had to be tended like any other important crop. By the eleventh century AD there was a huge silk industry in China.

Making silk by hand takes great skill. At the right time, the cocoons have to be plunged into hot water, and then the long threads are slowly unravelled.

The farmer plants out the rice seedlings in the flooded field. In the background, you can see the raised fields built on the side of a hill. By building these terraced fields, the Chinese could make more and more land productive.

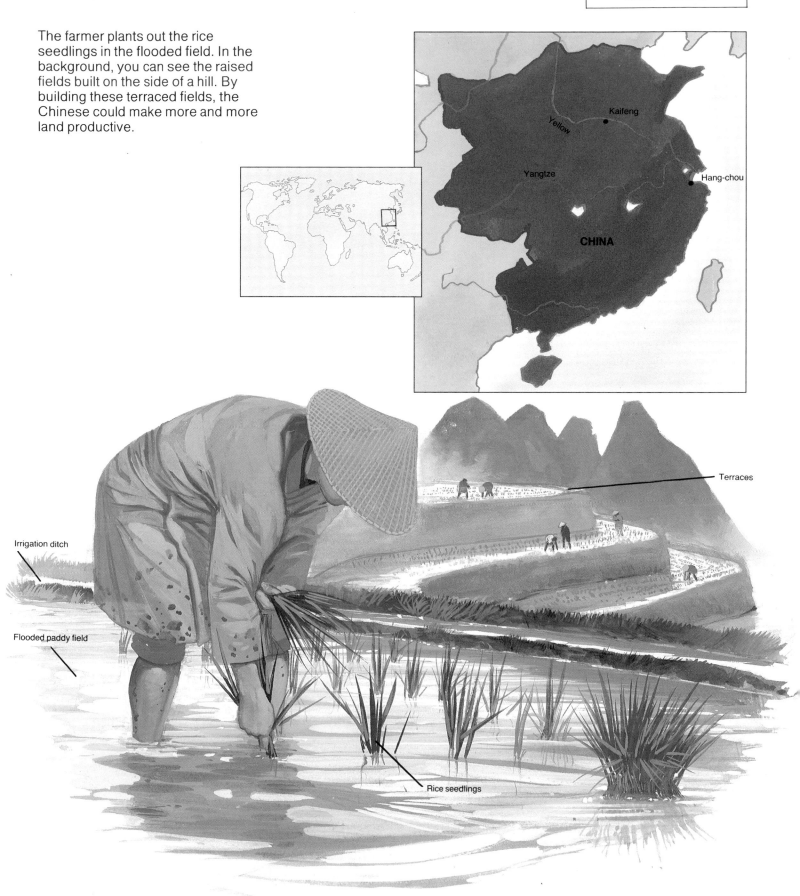

CHINA

Yellow

Kaifeng

Yangtze

Hang-chou

Terraces

Irrigation ditch

Flooded paddy field

Rice seedlings

23

A Chinese rice farmer

Wet rice growing was hard work, but produced a very good crop. One reason for this was the use of a flooded field. For the growing plants, the muddy water was like a rich soup, stirred up by the feet of the farmer and his water buffalo. Minerals floating in the water would release phosphorus, an important nutrient for the growing rice. In dry farming, nutrients often escape, into the air as gases or carried through the subsoil by rain-water. But a flooded field slows down this process.

In the eleventh century, the Chinese began to use early-ripening varieties of rice, which had been brought from *Champa* (modern Vietnam). The *Champa* rice took less time to ripen, so more crops could be planted.

Because they kept few animals, the farmers had to find other sources of fertilizer than animal manure. They used night-soil, human excrement which was collected from the towns in carts and brought to the countryside. Night-soil was a valuable article of trade. It was watered down and fed to the growing rice crop. As a result of the use of

fertilizers, the paddies did not have to be left fallow to recover their fertility. The farmers could gather the same bumper harvest, from the same field, year after year.

Wet rice farming was so efficient that it produced a population explosion.

> **Moving water**
> The Chinese had different ways of raising the water on to their paddy fields. One used a chain of troughs which scooped the water from a stream on to a higher field, or into a channel. It might be driven by a water-wheel in a river or by an ox, walking round and round, tied to a large horizontal wheel. These methods of moving water enabled the peasants to grow rice on high ground in fields cut into the side of the hill.

The 'dragon's backbone' used foot-power to raise water onto the field. The weighted pole in the background uses the same principle as the Egyptian *shaduf* on page 11.

Between 750 and 1100, the population doubled, from 50 to 100 million. There was a shift of population from the north of China, where most people practised dry farming of wheat and millet, to the Yangtze river valley with its wet rice fields.

This painting shows a Chinese governor making a tour of inspection of a flourishing farming district. It comes from a series of paintings made to flatter the governor, whose name was Chao Hsia.

Animals for eating

Cattle were kept only for their strength. The Chinese did not eat beef, because the ox was seen as the farmer's helper. Canals and ponds among the rice fields were used to raise water chestnuts and to keep fish and ducks. Pigs, ducks and fish were the most important sources of meat. Fish had a useful effect: they ate the larvae of the mosquitoes which cause malaria, a big problem in hot, watery areas.

The clans

Village life was organized by the clan, which was like a huge extended family. On the large estates, the clans founded charities to look after their poorer members. The clan might also pay for the education of the cleverest village children. Education was the key to a career in China's vast civil service. It was every family's ambition that one of its members might become an important government official.

The growth of wet rice farming was encouraged by the Sung emperors, who ruled China from 960 to 1279. The government encouraged the farmers to sow the new fast-growing rice and to use new machinery, such as a winnowing fan (used for separating grains from husks) which was operated by a hand crank. Each year, the emperor would start the farming season by setting his hands to a plough.

With such a good supply of rice, China became an important centre for trade, and soon market towns grew into cities. The biggest city of all was Kaifeng, the Sung capital. Kaifeng was built on a canal linking the Yellow River in the north with the Yangtze.

The city was the centre of an industrial region, where people made porcelain, iron tools, and silk and cotton textiles. This was a time of great wealth, especially for the merchants who set up trading houses on the banks of the Yangtze. But it was all made possible because the flooded paddy field produced such a good crop of rice.

An English serf

Serfs were peasant farmers who were neither fully free, nor slaves. They could not leave the village, sell an ox or marry without the lord of the manor's permission. Serfs had to pay for the right to farm their land by working for a set number of days on the lord's land. They also had to give part of their produce to the lord as rent.

The serf's land was made up of a number of narrow strips, scattered among three huge fields. Each field would have a different crop, which was rotated. One year wheat would be sown, the next year, barley; in the third year, the field would be left fallow so that the soil could recover. The serf needed strips in each of the fields to have a share of each year's harvest.

Beyond the fields were meadows, which provided hay; a large field, called a common, where cattle could graze; and woods where pigs could forage for nuts and roots.

The medieval plough

The most important farming tool was the heavy plough. It was fitted with a vertical iron blade called a coulter which cut a path for a horizontal blade called a ploughshare. A mouldboard would turn the soil and bury weeds at the same time. It needed four to eight oxen to pull it. This was beyond the means of individual serfs, so they worked as a team. One family would provide the plough while other families would each contribute an ox.

I saw a poor man hanging on to the plough. His coat was of coarse stuff, his hood was full of holes. As he trod the soil, his toes peered out of his worn shoes. He was covered with mud. He drove four heifers [young cows] before him that had become so feeble that men might count their every rib. (Pierce the Ploughman's Creed, anonymous poem written about 1394, lines 421–32)

The team pulls the heavy plough through the wet soil.

SCOTLAND

York

Nottingham

WALES

ENGLAND

London

Canterbury

Exeter

Team of oxen

Handle

Ploughshare

Coulter with iron tip

Mouldboard

An English serf

In 1300, almost everyone in Western Europe worked on the land. Towns were small and surrounded by fields and one of their most important features was a market where farmers could sell their produce. Even the people who lived in towns kept animals and planted vegetables.

Most people lived in villages, in small cottages which they often shared with their animals. These were timber framed and covered with wattle (woven twigs) and daub (straw and mud). There would only be one or two rooms, with a smoky fire at the centre. In a small garden at the back, the women would grow vegetables such as cabbages and onions. The main part of the diet was coarse bread, which was made at home and baked in the village oven. Each village would also have a windmill or watermill, owned by the lord of the manor, where the serfs were expected to pay to grind their grain.

The biggest building in the village would have been the parish church. Everyone belonged to the Catholic Church and religion was very important. By law, serfs had to give a tenth of their produce, called a tithe, to pay for the church's upkeep. On Sunday, which was a day of rest, everyone would be expected to go to church and listen to the service. Most of the serfs would not have understood it because it was in Latin – which was taught only to priests and some rich people.

The church was the centre of village life, the only place where everyone regularly met. It was where

A village in medieval times. There are three main fields, divided up into strips. Each family would have owned one or two strips in each field. On the left of the river is the common land, while on the far right is a wood.

In the Middle Ages, there was never enough hay to keep many animals alive during the winter months.

they were baptized, married and buried. It was where they gathered to celebrate the feasts of the Christian calendar and the farming year. For example, early in January every year, on Plough Monday, a plough would be brought into the church and blessed by the priest.

The walls of the church were richly decorated – there would often be a Doom Painting, which showed sinners being carried off to Hell while the

saved were welcomed into Heaven. Such paintings were the only works of art that most serfs saw.

Everyone in the village depended on everyone else. Under the strip system, they all planted the same crops at the same time. They harvested the

A thirteenth-century Doom Painting from Chaldon Church in Surrey, England. People who have been 'damned' fall down into Hellfire.

grain as a team. Their animals grazed together on the common outside the village. Everyone knew everyone else's business. Any disagreements they had would be settled at the manor court.

The strip-farming system was wasteful in many ways. The serfs would waste time moving from one strip to another. The spaces between strips could not be used and they were often covered with weeds which spread into the crop. Although the fallow field produced nothing, it still had to be ploughed. But it was a very reliable system, and lasted in most parts of England from before 1100 until about 1700.

A yam farmer of Benin

By the beginning of the sixteenth century the city of Benin in West Africa was the centre of the forest kingdom of the Edo people. Like the land of the Mayas, this was tropical rainforest, where the rainy season lasted for half of the year. Like the Mayas, the Edo people used a slash-and-burn method of farming. But instead of growing maize, their main crop was the yam.

Most of the Edo people lived in villages in the forests. They would farm in family groups in which men and women each had different tasks to perform. In January, men and boys would choose sites in the bush. During the next two months, they would clear a field using iron axes and knives, afterwards burning the bush. In March, at the beginning of the rains, they would hoe the ground and plant the cuttings from yam plants or small yam tubers – yam plants could grow from either of these. Then the women and girls would take over. They

This modern photograph from Ghana shows harvested yams piled up.

would weed the plots and plant other crops – beans, groundnuts and peppers. From mid-September to November, the yams would be harvested by men and women, working together.

Eating yams

A Dutchman called Nyendael, who visited Benin in the seventeenth century, described the use of the yam:

The common diet of the rich is beef, mutton or chicken, with yams, which take the place of bread; these they boil and beat very fine in order to make cakes of them. The poorer people, whose bread is also yams, bananas and beans, eat fish.

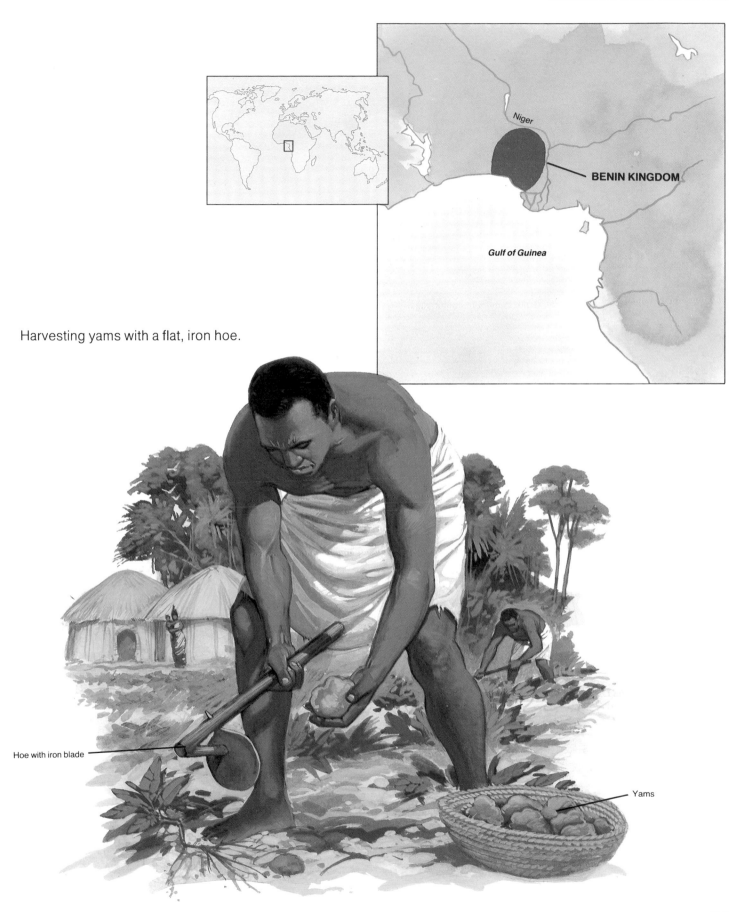

BENIN KINGDOM

Niger

Gulf of Guinea

Harvesting yams with a flat, iron hoe.

Hoe with iron blade

Yams

A yam farmer of Benin

Edo farming was similar in method to that of the Mayas. But the Edo had one thing which made their work easier – the knowledge of how to make iron axes and hoes. Iron blades stay sharper for longer than stone blades, and they can be made lighter and thinner than a stone axe or hoe. The village blacksmith was an important figure, a master of fire who was thought to have magical powers.

All the Edo people called themselves slaves of the *Oba*, or king, of Benin. They kept slaves of their own, captured in wars against other peoples. But only the Edo could be the slaves of the *Oba*. It was

considered an honour to belong to him.

The *Oba* was believed to be the protector of his people. He was like a priest and a magician combined. People believed that the *Oba* was able to speak to the gods and to the spirits of his dead ancestors. He had to perform special ceremonies to make sure that the rains came and that the harvest was good. Festivals were held in which slaves were

sacrificed to the sun and to the rain god.

The most important Edo festival was *agwe*, the feast of the new yams. This took place during the harvest season, in November. No one could eat any of the new yams until the ceremony had been performed. It would begin

This print from the early nineteenth century shows European visitors watching the great yam festival. It is thanks to the accounts left by Europeans that we know what happened during the festival.

with a procession to the palace with singing and dancing. A number of slaves and animals would be sacrificed. Then the *Oba* would take a newly harvested yam and place it in a pot which he would cover with soil. During further singing and dancing, the pot would be switched for one holding a larger yam. This would then be held up to show the people. It appeared as if the yam had magically grown in size. It was believed that the larger the yam had 'grown', the better the harvest would be.

Twice yearly, all the Edo villages had to send a tax to the *Oba* – yams, palm-oil, pepper and kola nuts. The *Oba*'s wealth came partly from this tax, partly from warfare and partly from trade. The Edo sold kola nuts to the peoples of North Africa; and palm oil (for soap), ivory, pepper and slaves to Europeans, who began to visit Benin after the 1480s. Only the *Oba* was allowed to trade with foreigners. He would send out his chiefs to the villages to organize the collection of whatever the traders needed.

In the Edo villages, all the men were divided into three different groups,

One of the bronze heads made by the Edo craftsmen for their *Oba*, or ruler. It shows the vertical scars which the Edo men made on their foreheads (in this case three scars just above the eye).

Edo art
The Edo were skilful artists and craftspeople, particularly in bronze or brass. They used a technique called lost wax casting. A clay sculpture would be covered in beeswax and then covered in plaster. Hot metal would be poured through a tube into the mould, melting the wax and filling the space it left. The metal casters worked only for the *Oba* and his palace was full of their work.

depending on their age. The most important people in the village were the elders, and the wisest of them would be the village head man. He was responsible for sorting out arguments and raising the tax for the *Oba*. The next group, the younger men, were liable to be called up to serve in the *Oba*'s army. He regularly waged war on neighbouring peoples, to capture slaves and collect taxes. The third group was made up of the youths of the village.

The Edo women often worked harder than the men. As well as looking after the vegetable crops and weeding the yams, they had to prepare the food and take produce to market. Edo men could have as many wives as they could afford to marry.

An improving farmer of Britain

In Britain, 1800 was the time of the gentleman farmer. In previous centuries, farming had been looked down on as work only fit for peasants. But in 1800 even King George III had a farm on his estates at Windsor. He was nicknamed 'Farmer George'. The hard work was still done by the poor, now working as wage labourers rather than serfs. But it was directed by wealthy landowners.

The reason for this change lay in a new interest in scientific farming methods. The gentlemen farmers, or improvers, experimented with different techniques to produce fatter animals, better soils and bigger crops.

Under the old open field system, everyone had planted the same crops at the same time, so new farming methods could never be tried. The farmers of 1800 were able to experiment because of enclosure. Under the enclosure system the huge

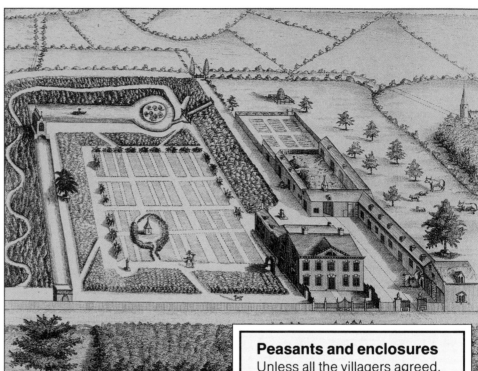

An engraving of the estate of a wealthy 'improver' in Leicestershire, England, in about 1750. It shows the house and garden, the farm, enclosed fields, parkland and woods.

open fields made up of narrow strips were replaced by farms with compact fields. The village common, where all the animals had grazed, was also divided up and enclosed. Land which had been farmed communally could now be farmed by individual improvers.

Peasants and enclosures

Unless all the villagers agreed, a landowner who wanted to enclose the fields would need a special law passed to allow it, called a private Act of Parliament. After such a law had been passed, inspectors called 'Parliamentary commissioners' would visit the village. They would redraw the map of the village fields. Each farmer would then be given a field that was the size of all his strips put together, with a little bit extra added to compensate the farmer because he could no longer use the common. The farmers would have to pay the commissioners and then pay for the hedging of their new fields. Poorer farmers who could not afford this often had to sell their farm.

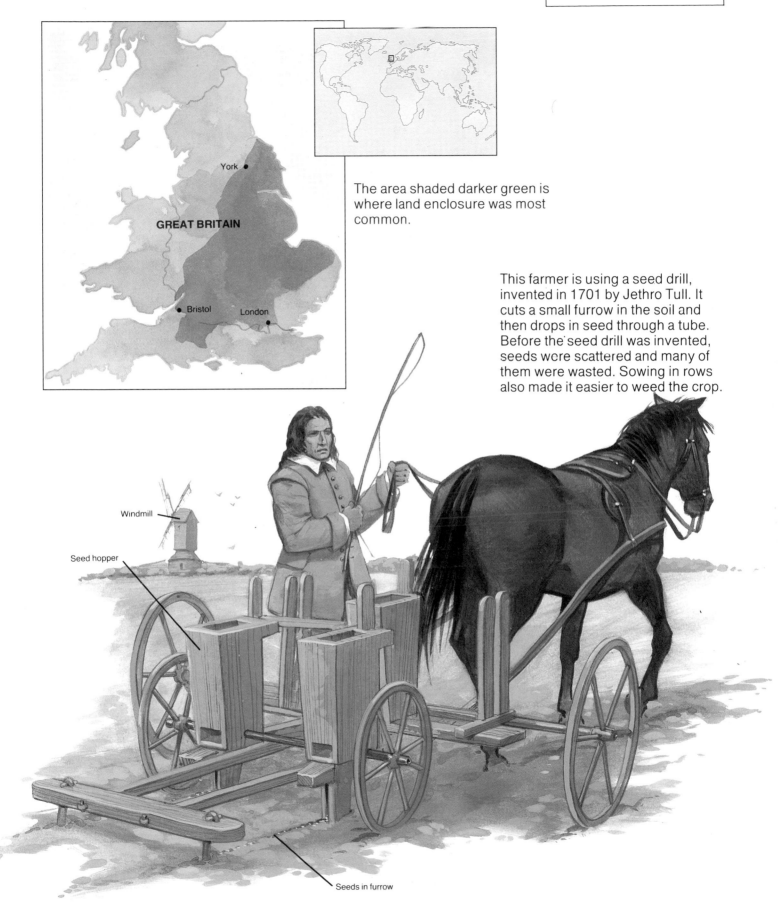

The area shaded darker green is where land enclosure was most common.

GREAT BRITAIN

York

Bristol   London

This farmer is using a seed drill, invented in 1701 by Jethro Tull. It cuts a small furrow in the soil and then drops in seed through a tube. Before the seed drill was invented, seeds were scattered and many of them were wasted. Sowing in rows also made it easier to weed the crop.

Windmill

Seed hopper

Seeds in furrow

During the eighteenth century, British farming went through what is called an agricultural revolution. This means that everything to do with farming changed, from the shape of the fields to the crops grown in them.

Most of the 'improving' actually occurred in England. In Scotland, large numbers of poor farmers, called crofters, were cleared off the land to make way for rich sheep farmers. In Ireland (ruled at this time by Britain) farming was not 'improved' and most farmers continued to try to live off what they could grow on the small plots they farmed.

One of the most important changes was the use of new combinations of crops to be grown in different years or 'rotated'. Previously, wheat and barley had been rotated. Lord 'Turnip' Townsend (1674–1738) was famous for adding turnips and clover (grown as cattle feed) to the crops. In this way, over four years the crop rotation for one field might be: year 1 wheat; year 2 turnips; year 3 barley or oats; year 4 clover. Turnips are root crops and use a different level of soil from cereals.

A Chinese breed of pig, widely used in England in the early nineteenth century as it fattened quickly.

The same village as shown on page 28, after enclosure. The large fields have been divided into smaller ones, edged with hedges, and the individual strips have disappeared. The common land, to the left of the river, has been divided into fields, and there are even new fields to the right of the church, on the edge of the wood.

Clover actually helps to keep goodness in the soil. So with the new rotations, fields did not have to be left fallow every third year. The soil would also be improved by the manure of the animals which ate the turnips and clover.

Farmers discovered ways of improving their soil by adding marl, a mixture of lime with clay or chalk. Clay marl, added to sandy soil, helped it hold water. Chalk marl was added to heavy clay soils to help drainage. As a result, more land could be used to grow bigger crops. With more cattle food being grown, more animals could now be kept alive throughout the winter. Now, fresh meat could be eaten all year round.

The increased demand for meat meant that farmers now wanted to breed heavier types of animal. They had previously wanted cattle with strong legs to pull the plough, and sheep with thick coats of wool. Under the open field system, all the animals had grazed together on the common, so selective breeding was not possible. But in the enclosed fields, farmers could control breeding and create new types of animal.

A country meeting of the Royal Agricultural Society. At such meetings the gentlemen farmers could see new inventions and learn about new methods.

The most famous of the animal improvers was Robert Bakewell (1725–95). He cross-bred different types of sheep and created the New Leicester, an animal which put on fat quickly (people liked fatty meat at this time). By 1800, many farmers were raising animals which were twice or three times the size of livestock in 1700.

New farming methods were needed in the eighteenth century because the population was growing fast. During George III's reign (1760–1820), the population of Britain (excluding Ireland) almost doubled, from 8 million to 14 million. But the poorest villagers suffered because of the new methods. They had few, if any, strips to farm and had scraped a living by grazing a cow and a few geese on the common. But the common was now enclosed and although the people were given tiny plots of land, these were often too small to be of use. Many left the countryside to work in the new factories. Others stayed to work as wage labourers for the gentlemen farmers.

A Soviet collective farmer

By 1937, most farmers in the Soviet Union worked on collective farms or kolkhozes. The kolkhozes were created by pooling together the land of all the peasants in a village. The land was then owned by the whole community.

The farmers were provided with new machinery by the government. Experts were sent to show them the lastest farming methods. In return, after each harvest, the collective farm had to hand over a certain amount of produce to the government.

This was a time of great change for the Soviet peasant farmer. Up until 1928, 70 per cent of the people in the Soviet Union lived as peasant farmers. They had used traditional farming methods, growing their crops in small strips like the serfs of medieval Europe. Many of the farmers had been so poor that they had to use wooden rather than iron ploughs. But the communist government, which had taken power in the Soviet Union in 1917, decided in 1928 that the peasants would have to learn to use modern farming methods, pooling all their land to form a collective farm.

Farmers from the Ukraine, signing an agreement between collective farms, in Moscow, 1929.

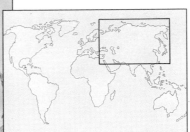

On the new farms, peasants who had previously worked only with their families had to learn to work and live with large groups of fellow peasants. These women workers, pictured in about 1930, are hoeing a field of cabbages on their State Farm.

A Soviet collective farmer

The decision to set up collective farms was part of a campaign to turn the Soviet Union into a modern industrial nation. The Soviet government needed money to buy factory equipment from other countries. The government decided that the best way to get hold of the money was by selling Soviet grain. But first they needed to increase the amount of grain produced so that they could sell the grain without starving their own people. The new factories could then build tractors to help the farmers. Grain was also needed to feed the growing populations of the factory towns.

The campaign to create collective farms began in 1928. At first, the government simply tried to persuade the peasants of the benefits of collective farming. Special trains were sent into the countryside equipped with mobile cinemas. Here the peasants watched films which showed the advantages of modern farming methods.

But most of the peasants hated the idea of losing their private property. They were also afraid that they would lose their

One of the first Soviet tractors, a crude machine started with a hand-crank. The instructor, in a light coat, is surrounded by peasants who have come to learn how to use it.

freedom if they joined a collective farm. They thought it would be like working in a factory. By 1929, only 4 per cent of the peasants had joined the kolkhozes. With the campaign of persuasion failing, the government decided to use force.

It was decided that the wealthier farmers – the kulaks – would be driven off their property. Between 1929 and 1931, over a million peasant families were rounded up and sent to labour camps. Their land was either given to a collective farm, or claimed by the government, and a state farm (*sovkhoz*) was set up. Local peasants would work on state farms as paid labourers.

To avoid being arrested, many peasants joined the new farms. But many desperately resisted. Rather than hand over their animals, the peasants slaughtered them for meat: half of the country's stock

---

The famine of 1932–3

Fedor Belov grew up on a collective farm. In 1956 he wrote about the famine of 1932–3:

The peasants ate dogs, horses, rotten potatoes, the bark of trees, grass – anything they could find. Incidents of cannibalism were not uncommon. The people were like wild beasts, ready to devour one another. And no matter what they did, they went on dying. They died singly and in families. They died everywhere – in the yards and on the trains. There was no one to bury them. I was thirteen years old then and I shall never forget what I saw. (The History of a Soviet Collective Farm)

40

of cattle, horses and sheep was destroyed between 1929 and 1933.

By 1931, more than half of all peasant households were in collective farms. But the new kolkhozes produced less grain in 1931 than the old farms had in 1928. The kulaks had been the most efficient of the farmers, but now they had gone.

Below Lunch-time on a collective farm in Russia, 1938. This photo was probably taken for propaganda purposes, to show other people that life on a kolkhoz was well-organized, and that there was plenty to eat.

Above The 1930s were a time of vast building projects in the Soviet Union, often using forced labour. These Uzbek workers are digging a canal.

The peasants who remained felt that they had no reason to work hard. Farmers were accused of hoarding grain for themselves, and armed squads were sent by the government to the farms to take grain by force.

As a result of the grain seizures, the countryside suffered a terrible famine in 1932–3. It is estimated that more than seven million peasants died of hunger. But the peasants who survived the famine decided to make the best of the new farming methods. By the end of 1937, about twenty-five million small farms had been replaced by a quarter of a million collective farms and state farms. In 1940, farms were producing 30 per cent more grain than in 1928.

A modern Western farmer

A modern farmer in places like the USA, Canada, Western Europe and Australia, has little in common with the farmers of the past. Almost all the tasks previously carried out by hand, or with the help of oxen or horses, are now performed by machines.

The key machine is the tractor, which can pull or push a variety of equipment such as a plough, a harrow for breaking up clods of earth, or a seed drill for planting. Also important is the combine harvester, which reaps, threshes, winnows and stores grain as it cuts a path through a field of wheat. One person driving a combine harvester can do work that in the past would have needed a whole community.

In modern farms, technology is also important for raising livestock, particularly pigs and chickens. These animals are now raised intensively – this means that large numbers of them are now kept in huge farm buildings, where food and temperature can be carefully controlled.

Many modern farmers use a range of chemicals to improve their produce. Fertilizers are used to help crops grow, and herbicides and pesticides are used to kill off weeds and insects that might damage the crop. Animals are now given drugs called vaccines to prevent them falling ill. If they do fall ill, they may be cured with medicines called antibiotics.

Modern tractors can be fitted with attachments allowing them to pull several ploughs at once. Ploughing a field on one of the huge farms of Pennsylvania in the USA.

Farming and the landscape

The tools a farmer uses give the fields their shape. In 1300, a medieval serf's strips were a furlong (a furrow long, 201 metres), because this was the distance a team of oxen could pull a plough without resting. Nowadays a combine harvester and a tractor have no such limitations. As a result, the modern farmer can grow crops in vast fields.

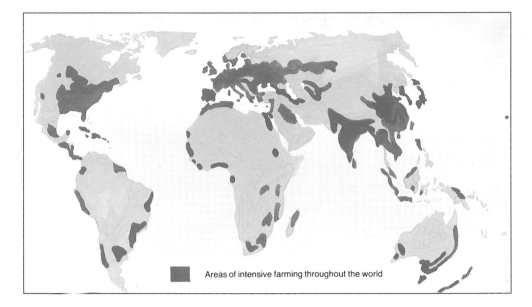

Areas of intensive farming throughout the world

Helicopters and planes are now used
to spray crops with pesticides.

Spray nozzles

Herbicide or pesticide spray —

Although modern farming can produce more food than ever before, it has created a series of new problems. In the USA and Western Europe, farmers can now grow so much grain that they cannot always sell it at a profit. Sometimes this food is bought up by governments and stored in 'food mountains'. Sometimes the food is simply left to rot.

Now that farmers can increase the fertility of their fields with artificial chemicals, they no longer depend on cattle, sheep and pig manure to keep the fields fertile. As a result, mixed farming, combining crops and livestock, has become much less common. With livestock raised intensively in buildings instead of outside in fields, there is a problem with getting rid of their waste. The slurry (dung, urine and water) from modern farmyards can pollute neighbouring streams and rivers. Rivers can also be polluted by fertilizers. If it rains immediately after a farmer has spread fertilizer over the fields, the fertilizer may be washed straight into a stream or lake. This may result in fish and plant life dying. Pesticides are also blamed for killing not only pests, but many different animals and plants.

The treatment of animals has also been criticized. Some people have campaigned against chickens and turkeys being kept in crowded sheds, and pigs being kept in cramped stalls where they cannot even turn around. Farmers point out, though, that all these measures are used to keep costs down and provide cheap food for the consumer.

In the 1980s, there were a series of 'food scares' when people worried that intensive farming methods might produce food which caused ill health. The practice of recycling chicken carcasses as chicken food was blamed for the appearance of a dangerous form of food poisoning, *salmonella enteriditis*, in eggs. When the problem was recognized, many poultry farmers went out of business as sales of eggs fell dramatically.

Some farmers have rejected the use of chemicals and switched to organic farming, using crop rotations to keep down pests, animal manure for fertilizer and herbal remedies instead of

Food from around the world

Thanks to refrigeration and modern transport, farmers can now sell fresh vegetables and fruit in distant countries. Fruit and vegetables can be packed in refrigerated containers, which are kept at carefully controlled temperatures. If everything goes well the fruit and vegetables do not ripen until they reach the shops. The refrigerated containers can be transported by road, rail or sea. Valuable crops, such as avocados, are sometimes transported by air. Next time you visit a supermarket, see how many different countries have produced the fruit and vegetables on sale.

Intensive farming

Poultry and pigs are kept in huge sheds, where heating, lighting and even feeding is carefully controlled. Chickens reared for laying eggs are kept in battery cages, feeding from a trough and laying their eggs directly on to a conveyor belt. Broiler chickens, raised for meat, are kept in huge numbers in sheds. In the 1960s, it took 84 days to rear a broiler chicken ready for slaughter. Now, it takes only 42 days, exactly half the time. As a result, chicken meat has become much cheaper.

Left Very young chickens are delivered into a poultry shed, to be raised where temperature, light, food and water are all carefully controlled.

Below A giant machine harvests sugar cane in North Queensland, Australia. The harvester deposits the sugar-filled stems of the cane into a trailer, which is pulled along by a tractor at the same speed; the useless chaff and leaves are blown away in the breeze.

antibiotics to treat sick animals. Organic farming is less productive than intensive farming (for example, a field of wheat farmed organically will only produce half the crop grown using chemicals). Because organic farming is less productive, the crops produced cost more. But many people are prepared to pay more for food free of chemicals, produced without cruelty to animals.

Glossary

Archaeologist Someone who studies the way people lived in the past by looking at the places they lived in and the objects they used.

Billhook A cutting tool with a wooden handle and a curved blade, which ends in a hook.

Blacksmith Someone who makes or repairs things made of iron.

Breed To allow farm animals to mate and so maintain or increase their number. Selective breeding means mating animals with certain characteristics, such as a woolly coat or extra fat.

Canal An artificial waterway built for irrigation or to allow boats to navigate inland.

Cereal Any type of grass which produces grain which we can eat; for instance: wheat, barley, maize, rice, oats, rye, sorghum and millet.

Ceremony An important event, such as a wedding, which is always carried out in the same way.

Domesticate To bring animals and plants under human control. Full domestication occurs when an animal or plant comes to depend on people so much that it could not survive in the wild.

Drought A long period of dry weather.

Estate A large area of land with one owner.

Fallow Land which is rested to recover its goodness.

Fertile soil Plants need fertile soil to be able to grow properly. Nutrients (see entry) make the soil fertile. Without them plants will either not grow properly, or they will not grow at all.

Fertilizer Any substance mixed into soil to make it fertile.

Flint A type of stone which when broken up produces flakes with very sharp edges. In prehistoric times, knives and other tools were made of flint.

Grain The fruit of a grass plant. Grain can be ground to make flour.

Hoe A tool for digging and weeding, with a blade made of flint, metal or wood, attached to a straight handle.

Husk The outer covering of a seed. Grain husks are usually removed before the grain can be used.

Irrigation The supply of water to dry areas.

Manure Animal excrement, usually mixed with straw, used to fertilize land.

Nutrient Any of the mineral substances that are absorbed by the roots of plants and are necessary for the plant's growth.

Paddy field A flooded field, used for growing wet rice.

Peasant farmer Someone who lives off crops grown on a small farm.

Pest An animal or insect that feeds on crops. Pesticides are chemicals used to kill them.

Plough A tool for cutting furrows in the soil, pulled by oxen or horses.

Pollute To spoil or make dirty.

Population The number of people living in a particular place.

Rotation Growing a series of different crops, one after the other, in the same field. It reduces the threat from pests and disease and helps the soil to stay fertile.

Sacrifice An offering to a god. In some religions it is thought necessary to give up something valuable as a sacrifice.

Sickle A cutting tool with a curved blade and a short handle.

Slaughter To kill a farm animal so that it can be eaten.

Threshing Beating or rubbing grain, to separate it from the rest of the harvested plant, either on a threshing floor or in a threshing machine.

Winnowing Separating grains from the straw and outer skins or husks (the chaff) by fanning them, or tossing them in the wind.

Further reading

Early People (Dorling Kindersley, 1989)

Skipp, Victor, *Out of the Ancient World* (Penguin, 1967)

Hart, George, *Ancient Egypt* (Dorling Kindersley, 1990)

Oliphant, Margaret, *The Egyptian World* (Kingfisher Books, 1989)

James, Simon, *Ancient Rome* (Dorling Kindersley 1990)

Corbishly, Mike, *The Roman World* (Kingfisher Books, 1986)

Nicholson, Robert, and Watts, Claire, *Ancient China* (Two-can Publishing, 1991)

Ross, Stewart, *A Medieval Serf* (Wayland 1985)

Ormrod, Mark, *Life in the Middle Ages* (Wayland, 1991)

Martin, Christopher, *Spotlight on the Agricultural Revolution* (Wayland, 1986)

Addy, John, *The Agrarian Revolution* (Longman, 1964)

Gibson, Michael, *Russia under Stalin* (Wayland, 1972)

On modern farming:

Becklake, Sue, *Food and Farming* (Aladdin Books, 1989)

Lambert, Mark, *Farming Technology* (Wayland, 1990)

Rickard, G., *Twentieth Century Farming* (Wayland, 1988)

Timeline

Periods covered in this book and some of the major developments in farming.

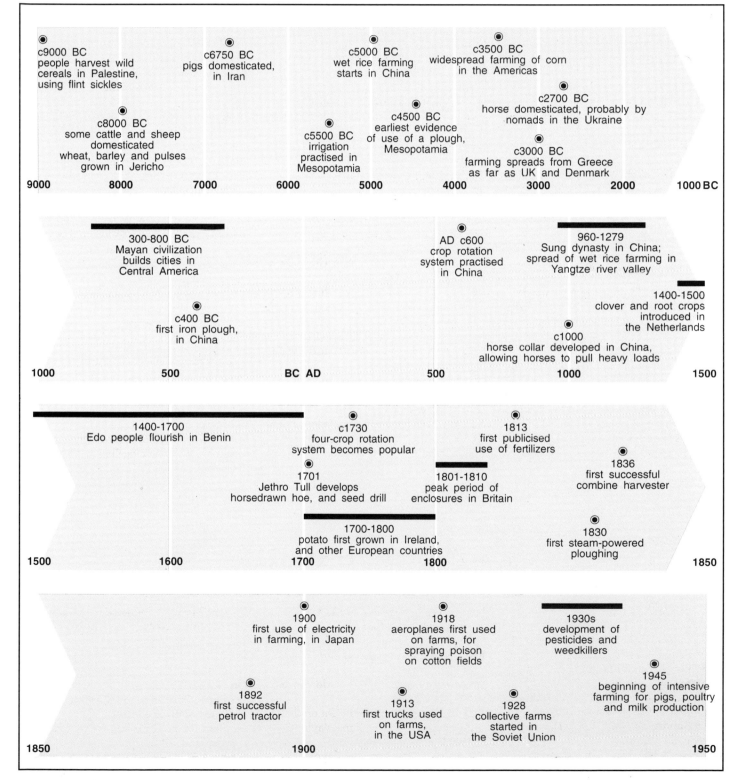

c9000 BC people harvest wild cereals in Palestine, using flint sickles

c6750 BC pigs domesticated, in Iran

c5000 BC wet rice farming starts in China

c3500 BC widespread farming of corn in the Americas

c8000 BC some cattle and sheep domesticated wheat, barley and pulses grown in Jericho

c5500 BC irrigation practised in Mesopotamia

c4500 BC earliest evidence of use of a plough, Mesopotamia

c2700 BC horse domesticated, probably by nomads in the Ukraine

c3000 BC farming spreads from Greece as far as UK and Denmark

9000   8000   7000   6000   5000   4000   3000   2000   1000 BC

300-800 BC Mayan civilization builds cities in Central America

AD c600 crop rotation system practised in China

960-1279 Sung dynasty in China; spread of wet rice farming in Yangtze river valley

c400 BC first iron plough, in China

1400-1500 clover and root crops introduced in the Netherlands

c1000 horse collar developed in China, allowing horses to pull heavy loads

1000   500   BC AD   500   1000   1500

1400-1700 Edo people flourish in Benin

c1730 four-crop rotation system becomes popular

1813 first publicised use of fertilizers

1701 Jethro Tull develops horsedrawn hoe, and seed drill

1801-1810 peak period of enclosures in Britain

1836 first successful combine harvester

1700-1800 potato first grown in Ireland, and other European countries

1830 first steam-powered ploughing

1500   1600   1700   1800   1850

1900 first use of electricity in farming, in Japan

1918 aeroplanes first used on farms, for spraying poison on cotton fields

1930s development of pesticides and weedkillers

1945 beginning of intensive farming for pigs, poultry and milk production

1892 first successful petrol tractor

1913 first trucks used on farms, in the USA

1928 collective farms started in the Soviet Union

1850   1900   1950

47

Index

Sources of quotations

Page 12: The quote on an Egyptian peasant is from *Out of the Ancient World* by Victor Skipp, Penguin Books, 1967, pp. 74-5. Page 13: T.G.H. James quotes the god *Khnum* in *Myths and Legends of Ancient Egypt*, Hamlyn Publishing, 1969, p. 97. Page 14: the two extracts on a slave's life are from *Marcus Porcius Cato on Agriculture; Marcus Terentius Varro on Agriculture* (with an English translation by W.D. Hooper), Loeb Classical Library, Heinemann, 1960, pp. 7 and 225-7. Page 17: Pliny's *Natural History*, translated by H. Rackham is also published by Loeb Classical Library, Heinemann, 1950, p. 375. Page 26: A modern English version of *Pierce the Ploughman's Creed*, translated by H.S. Bennett is quoted by Anne Fuller in *Economy and Society in Western Europe 1300-1600*, Open University Press, 1971, pp. 8-9. Page 30: Nyendael on yam eating is to be found in *Great Benin: Its Customs, Art and Horrors* by H.L. Roth, 1903, reprinted by Routledge and Kegan Paul, 1968, pp. 147-8. Page 40: *The History of a Soviet Collective Farm* by Fedor Belov, Routledge and Kegan Paul, 1956, pp. 12-13.